I0828102

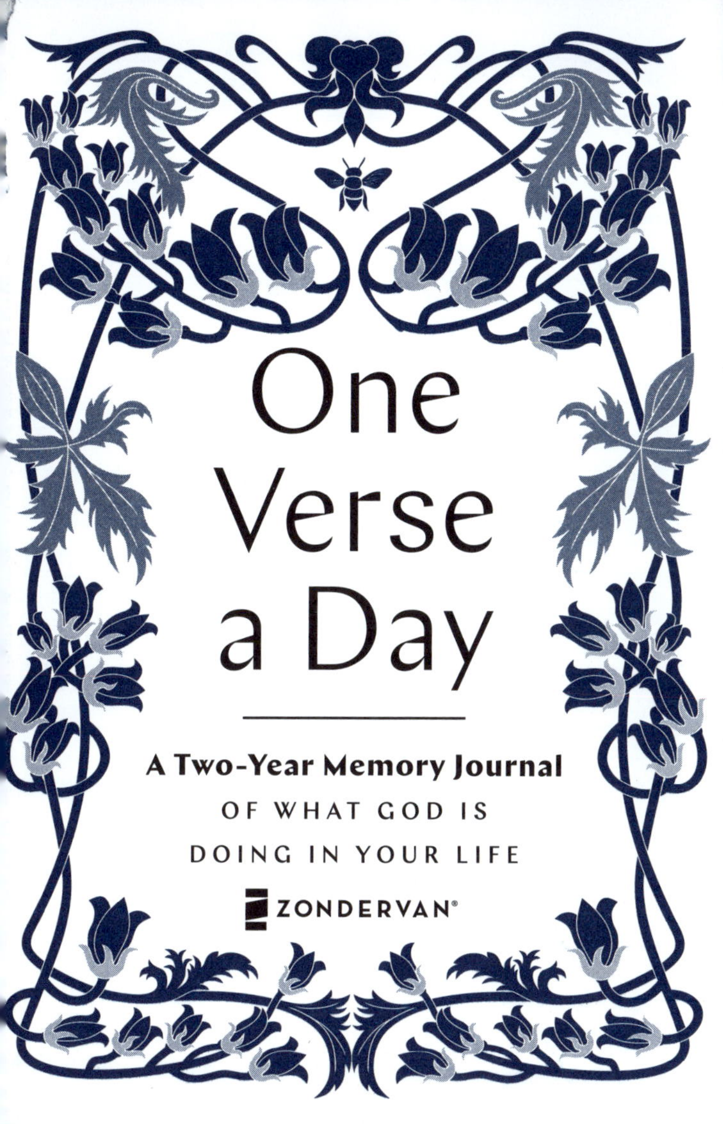

One Verse a Day

A Two-Year Memory Journal

OF WHAT GOD IS DOING IN YOUR LIFE

ZONDERVAN®

ZONDERVAN

One Verse a Day

Published by Zondervan, 3950 Sparks Drive SE, Suite 101, Grand Rapids, MI 49546, USA. Zondervan is a registered trademark of The Zondervan Corporation, L.L.C., a wholly owned subsidiary of HarperCollins Christian Publishing, Inc.

Requests for information should be addressed to customercare@harpercollins.com.

Zondervan titles may be purchased in bulk for educational, business, fundraising, or sales promotional use. For information, please email SpecialMarkets@Zondervan.com.

ISBN 978-0-310-46727-4 (HC)

Published in association with literary agent Maria Ribas of Stonesong, a literary agency and book packaging company. www.stonesong.com.

The Thomas Merton quote in the introduction is from *Thoughts in Solitude* (Farrar, Straus and Giroux, 1999).

HarperCollins Publishers, Macken House, 39/40 Mayor Street Upper, Dublin 1, D01 C9W8, Ireland (https://www.harpercollins.com)

Cover and interior design by Sabryna Lugge and Maria Ribas, Stonesong

Printed in India

25 26 27 28 29 REP 5 4 3 2 1

Presented to
From

Introduction
What Is Memory Journaling?

God is always working. But our memories aren't—we forget, we move on, we overlook the holy story unfolding each day. As each calendar page falls to the ground, we risk losing a page of our story—of God's story—that could be inserted in our book of life.

This journal is about capturing the beauty and glory of God's work as it's happening, day by day. It provides a place to record whatever is stirring in our hearts that day—anything from the gloriously boring coffee run of the morning to the days that push us to heartrending new realities. All parts of our story matter, and often it's in looking back at the small details of an ordinary day that we can most see what God is doing for us and in us.

But more than just a journal of the everyday, memory journaling opens a window into quiet, slowness, and time spent with God. This isn't about committing to a daily practice of journaling and believing that there's something lazy or wrong with you if you can't keep up with it. After all, how many of us have added "Start a daily journal" to our New Year's resolutions only to watch it become just another source of guilt, disappointment, and pressure?

What does it look like to make time for your best friend?

Life serves us up plenty of struggle as it is, so let's not pile onto ourselves. Instead, we hope you'll think about how you want to be in relationship with God each day. What does it look like to make time for your best friend, and what do you want to do together? Some days you'll want to read your Bible to feel connected to God; other days you'll want to take a prayer walk together; and sometimes you'll want to lie down and just be together in comfortable silence. Any of these ways of connecting to God is still part of the way He's working in you and worth memorializing in your journal.

Remember that God isn't worried about our streaks or letdowns, our moments when we nail it and when we fall flat. He just wants to be with us. On the next few pages you'll find some ways this journal can help you step into a few minutes of soul-soothing, quality time with your Creator.

A Menu of Options

for How to Use This Book

READ

Let God Guide the Way

Let God guide you to a verse. Open your Bible to a random spot and see what catches your eye. You might find that God has delivered up a verse that is exactly what you need that day. (He's good like that.) If not, keep reading through the page until something speaks to you and nudges a bit of movement in your spirit.

Go to a Favorite Book

Nestle into the comfort of a favorite book or passage and let the soft rhythm of the words flow over you. Allow the familiar outlines of the paragraphs to fill you with the joy, peace, or hope that has always met you in those lines.

Read in Order

Pick a starting point (it doesn't have to be Genesis) and begin reading through in order. Sometimes we discover that it's the "before" and the "after" moments surrounding the big stories that most resonate with what life feels like in all its glorious boringness. Let the in-between moments in the Bible fill the in-between moments in your day with meaning and peace.

See What Bubbles Up in You

If you have a verse pulling at your sleeve, dedicate that day to reflecting on it. God puts verses on our hearts at specific times for specific reasons, and slowing down to listen and discern what to do can provide the clarity and purpose we need throughout our day.

Invite Christ into Your Emotions

If you're a flurry of emotions—whether it's the frenzy of a busy day, the sadness of a disappointment, or the anger of an injustice—pause and name what you're feeling. Once you've named the emotion or issue, turn to the Verse Library and find out what God has to say about it. Invite Christ into your emotions, and let Him do the work in you that He wants to do.

Let Others Inspire You

If a verse comes your way during the day through a sermon, a friend's text, or any other way, give that verse space to work in your heart. God placed it in your path for a reason, and this practice will help you clear space and time to listen to what His Word has to give you.

WRITE

Freewrite

Let it all out—the lament, the joy, the fear—knowing that both God and this journal are expansive enough to hold it all. God cares about your smallest pinpricks and your largest aches, and it's in these details that we see Him at work.

Record

Write what God has done in your life that day or what you hope He will do in the day ahead. Writing your truest longings and fears and offering them up to God is pure intimacy with Him. And a month or a year from now, you can look back and see His movement in both your heart and your life.

Praise

As Thomas Merton wrote, "For the grateful person knows that God is good, not by hearsay but by experience. And that is what makes all the difference." Thank God for His goodness, for the gift of another day, and for the small and big things.

If You Get Stuck or Feel Resistance

We all get stuck in ruts sometimes, and we all feel resistance to slowing down and tuning into God. It's okay. Here are a few nudges to help you.

1. Try a movement practice.

Tuck your journal under your arm or in a bag and go for a walk with God. Talk to Him about your resistance and your fears, and let Him walk alongside you through it all. Find a spot to sit or stand still for a bit and journal all the prayers, pleas, and praises that come up as you walk.

2. Ask God some questions.

God is a God of answers, and we are a people of questions. Ask Him whatever is on your mind and heart that day. Open your Bible, open the ears of your heart, and listen to what He has to say. Two questions we've found helpful:

God, what do You want me to know?
God, what do You want me to do?

3. Sink into the comfort of His words.

Some days what you most need may be to copy a favorite prayer or passage into your journal. Even this can strengthen your communion with God if you focus mindfully on each pen stroke. And sometimes just letting the Word wash over you is exactly the way God wanted to work in you.

Verse Library

Here you'll find one hundred verses to inspire your prayer journaling. You can go directly to whatever topic is on your heart that day, or just scan through and see where God guides you. If you simply need to meditate on the Word, use your journaling space to slowly write the verse.

Anger

Proverbs 14:29: Whoever is patient has great understanding, but one who is quick-tempered displays folly.

Ephesians 4:26: In your anger do not sin: Do not let the sun go down while you are still angry.

Also: Psalm 103:8, Proverbs 12:16, James 1:19

Anxiety

Psalm 55:22: Cast your cares on the Lord and he will sustain you; he will never let the righteous be shaken.

Psalm 56:3: When I am afraid, I put my trust in you.

Also: Isaiah 35:4, Matthew 6:25, Philippians 4:13

Comfort

Psalm 119:76: May your unfailing love be my comfort.

Matthew 11:28: Come to me, all you who are weary and burdened, and I will give you rest.

Also: Psalm 23:6, Isaiah 49:13, John 16:33

Forgiveness

Psalm 103:12: As far as the east is from the west, so far has he removed our transgressions from us.

Luke 6:37: Do not judge, and you will not be judged. Do not condemn, and you will not be condemned. Forgive, and you will be forgiven.

Also: Mark 11:25, Luke 6:27, Ephesians 4:32

Gratitude

Psalm 118:24: The Lord has done it this very day; let us rejoice today and be glad.

John 11:41: So they took away the stone. Then Jesus looked up and said, "Father, I thank you that you have heard me."

Also: Psalm 100:4, Psalm 136:1, 2 Corinthians 9:11

Grief

Psalm 56:8: Record my misery; list my tears on your scroll—are they not in your record?

Matthew 5:4: Blessed are those who mourn, for they will be comforted.

Also: Psalm 31:9–10, Psalm 34:18, Psalm 73:26

Growth

Galatians 6:9: Let us not become weary in doing good, for at the proper time we will reap a harvest if we do not give up.

Ephesians 4:15: Instead, speaking the truth in love, we will grow to become in every respect the mature body of . . . Christ.

Also: Luke 8:14–15, Colossians 1:10, 2 Peter 3:18

Healing

Psalm 147:3: He heals the brokenhearted and binds up their wounds.

Jeremiah 17:14: Heal me, LORD, and I will be healed; save me and I will be saved, for you are the one I praise.

Also: Psalm 30:2, Psalm 6:2, Proverbs 4:20–22

Hope

Psalm 119:114: You are my refuge and my shield; I have put my hope in your word.

Lamentations 3:24: I say to myself, "The Lord is my portion; therefore I will wait for him."

Also: Psalm 42:11, Proverbs 23:18, Romans 8:24–25

Joy

Psalm 16:11: You make known to me the path of life; you will fill me with joy in your presence, with eternal pleasures at your right hand.

Romans 14:17: For the kingdom of God is not a

matter of eating and drinking, but of righteousness, peace and joy in the Holy Spirit.
Also: Psalm 4:7, John 16:22, 1 Peter 1:8

Justice

Isaiah 1:17: Learn to do right; seek justice. Defend the oppressed. Take up the cause of the fatherless; plead the case of the widow.
Micah 6:8: And what does the Lord require of you? To act justly and to love mercy and to walk humbly with your God.
Also: Psalm 37:27, Proverbs 18:5, Amos 5:24

Love

1 Corinthians 16:14: Do everything in love.
1 John 4:8: Whoever does not love does not know God, because God is love.
Also: John 3:16, 1 Corinthians 13:4–8, 1 Peter 4:8

Mercy

Psalm 23:6: Surely your goodness and love will follow me all the days of my life, and I will dwell in the house of the LORD forever.
James 2:13: Because judgment without mercy will be shown to anyone who has not been merciful. Mercy triumphs over judgment.
Also: Psalm 25:6, Matthew 5:7, Hebrews 4:16

Protection

Psalm 17:8: Keep me as the apple of your eye; hide me in the shadow of your wings.

Proverbs 18:10: The name of the LORD is a fortified tower; the righteous run to it and are safe.

Also: Exodus 14:14, Psalm 91:1–16, Nahum 1:7

Rest

Psalm 127:2: In vain you rise early and stay up late, toiling for food to eat—for he grants sleep to those he loves.

Mark 6:31: He said to them, "Come with me by yourselves to a quiet place and get some rest."

Also: Exodus 33:14, Psalm 46:10, Jeremiah 31:25

Self-Control

Proverbs 25:28: Like a city whose walls are broken through is a person who lacks self-control.

2 Timothy 1:7: For the Spirit God gave us does not make us timid, but gives us power, love and self-discipline.

Also: Romans 12:2, Ephesians 6:12, Titus 1:8

Trust

Psalm 56:3–4: When I am afraid, I put my trust in you. . . . What can mere mortals do to me?

Proverbs 3:5–6: Trust in the Lord with all your heart and lean not on your own understanding.

Also: Psalm 20:7, Psalm 31:14-15, Luke 16:10

January 1

20___ ___________________________

20___ ___________________________

January 2

20___ ___________________________

20___ ___________________________

God, show me where You're working.

January 3

20___ ________________________

____

____

____

20___ ________________________

____

____

____

January 4

20___ ________________________

____

____

____

20___ ________________________

____

____

____

Help me to see You in everything, Lord.

January 5

20___ ______________________________

____

____

____

20___ ______________________________

____

____

____

January 6

20___ ______________________________

____

____

____

20___ ______________________________

____

____

____

God, show me where You're working.

January 7

20___ ______________________________

____

____

____

20___ ______________________________

____

____

____

January 8

20___ ______________________________

____

____

____

20___ ______________________________

____

____

____

Help me to see You in everything, Lord.

January 9

20___ ______________________________

____

____

____

20___ ______________________________

____

____

____

January 10

20___ ______________________________

____

____

____

20___ ______________________________

____

____

____

God, show me where You're working.

January 11

20___ ______________________________

____

____

____

20___ ______________________________

____

____

____

January 12

20___ ______________________________

____

____

____

20___ ______________________________

____

____

____

Help me to see You in everything, Lord.

All the days
ordained for me
were written in
your book before
one of them
came to be.

Psalm 139:16

January 13

20___ ____________________________

____

____

____

20___ ____________________________

____

____

____

January 14

20___ ____________________________

____

____

____

20___ ____________________________

____

____

____

Help me to see You in everything, Lord.

January 15

20___ ____

____

____

____

20___ ____

____

____

____

January 16

20___ ____

____

____

____

20___ ____

____

____

____

God, show me where You're working.

January 17

20___ ______________________________

____

____

____

20___ ______________________________

____

____

____

January 18

20___ ______________________________

____

____

____

20___ ______________________________

____

____

____

Help me to see You in everything, Lord.

January 19

20___ ________________________________

20___ ________________________________

January 20

20___ ________________________________

20___ ________________________________

God, show me where You're working.

January 21

20___ ____________________________________

____

____

____

20___ ____________________________________

____

____

____

January 22

20___ ____________________________________

____

____

____

20___ ____________________________________

____

____

____

Help me to see You in everything, Lord.

January 23

20___ ______________________________

____

____

____

20___ ______________________________

____

____

____

January 24

20___ ______________________________

____

____

____

20___ ______________________________

____

____

____

God, show me where You're working.

January 25

20___ ______________________________

____

____

____

20___ ______________________________

____

____

____

January 26

20___ ______________________________

____

____

____

20___ ______________________________

____

____

____

Help me to see You in everything, Lord.

January 27

20___ ___________________________

____

____

____

20___ ___________________________

____

____

____

January 28

20___ ___________________________

____

____

____

20___ ___________________________

____

____

____

God, show me where You're working.

January 29

20___ ______________________________

____

____

____

20___ ______________________________

____

____

____

January 30

20___ ______________________________

____

____

____

20___ ______________________________

____

____

____

Help me to see You in everything, Lord.

January 31

20___

20___

February 1

20___

20___

God, show me where You're working.

February 2

20___ ____________________

____

____

____

20___ ____________________

____

____

____

February 3

20___ ____________________

____

____

____

20___ ____________________

____

____

____

Help me to see You in everything, Lord.

February 4

20___ ______________________________

____

____

____

20___ ______________________________

____

____

____

February 5

20___ ______________________________

____

____

____

20___ ______________________________

____

____

____

God, show me where You're working.

February 6

20___ ______________________________

____

____

____

20___ ______________________________

____

____

____

February 7

20___ ______________________________

____

____

____

20___ ______________________________

____

____

____

Help me to see You in everything, Lord.

February 8

20___ ____________________________

____

____

____

20___ ____________________________

____

____

____

February 9

20___ ____________________________

____

____

____

20___ ____________________________

____

____

____

God, show me where You're working.

February 10

20___ ______________________________

____

____

____

20___ ______________________________

____

____

____

February 11

20___ ______________________________

____

____

____

20___ ______________________________

____

____

____

Help me to see You in everything, Lord.

February 12

20___ ______________________________

____

____

____

20___ ______________________________

____

____

____

February 13

20___ ______________________________

____

____

____

20___ ______________________________

____

____

____

God, show me where You're working.

February 14

20___

20___

February 15

20___

20___

Help me to see You in everything, Lord.

February 16

20___ ______________________________

____

____

____

20___ ______________________________

____

____

____

February 17

20___ ______________________________

____

____

____

20___ ______________________________

____

____

____

God, show me where You're working.

February 18

20___ ______________________________

____

____

____

20___ ______________________________

____

____

____

February 19

20___ ______________________________

____

____

____

20___ ______________________________

____

____

____

Help me to see You in everything, Lord.

February 20

20___

20___

February 21

20___

20___

God, show me where You're working.

February 22

20___

20___

February 23

20___

20___

Help me to see You in everything, Lord.

February 24

20___

20___

February 25

20___

20___

God, show me where You're working.

February 26

20___ ______________________________

____

____

____

20___ ______________________________

____

____

____

February 27

20___ ______________________________

____

____

____

20___ ______________________________

____

____

____

Help me to see You in everything, Lord.

February 28

20___ ______________________________

____

____

____

20___ ______________________________

____

____

____

February 29

20___ ______________________________

____

____

____

20___ ______________________________

____

____

____

God, show me where You're working.

March 1

20___ ______________________________

____

____

____

20___ ______________________________

____

____

____

March 2

20___ ______________________________

____

____

____

20___ ______________________________

____

____

____

Help me to see You in everything, Lord.

March 3

20___ ______________________________

____

____

____

20___ ______________________________

____

____

____

March 4

20___ ______________________________

____

____

____

20___ ______________________________

____

____

____

God, show me where You're working.

March 5

20___ ______________________________

____

____

____

20___ ______________________________

____

____

____

March 6

20___ ______________________________

____

____

____

20___ ______________________________

____

____

____

Help me to see You in everything, Lord.

March 7

20___ ___________________________________

20___ ___________________________________

March 8

20___ ___________________________________

20___ ___________________________________

God, show me where You're working.

March 9

20___ ________________________________

____

____

____

20___ ________________________________

____

____

____

March 10

20___ ________________________________

____

____

____

20___ ________________________________

____

____

____

Help me to see You in everything, Lord.

March 11

20___ ________________________________

____

____

____

20___ ________________________________

____

____

____

March 12

20___ ________________________________

____

____

____

20___ ________________________________

____

____

____

God, show me where You're working.

March 13

20___

20___

March 14

20___

20___

Help me to see You in everything, Lord.

March 15

20___ ______________________________

____

____

____

20___ ______________________________

____

____

____

March 16

20___ ______________________________

____

____

____

20___ ______________________________

____

____

____

God, show me where You're working.

March 17

20___ ______________________________

____

____

____

20___ ______________________________

____

____

____

March 18

20___ ______________________________

____

____

____

20___ ______________________________

____

____

____

Help me to see You in everything, Lord.

March 19

20___ ______________________________

20___ ______________________________

March 20

20___ ______________________________

20___ ______________________________

God, show me where You're working.

March 21

20___ ______________________________

____

____

____

20___ ______________________________

____

____

____

March 22

20___ ______________________________

____

____

____

20___ ______________________________

____

____

____

Help me to see You in everything, Lord.

March 23

20___

20___

March 24

20___

20___

God, show me where You're working.

March 25

20___ ______________________________

____

____

____

20___ ______________________________

____

____

____

March 26

20___ ______________________________

____

____

____

20___ ______________________________

____

____

____

Help me to see You in everything, Lord.

March 27

20___ ______________________________

____

____

____

20___ ______________________________

____

____

____

March 28

20___ ______________________________

____

____

____

20___ ______________________________

____

____

____

God, show me where You're working.

Your word is a
lamp for my feet, a
light on my path.

Psalm 119:105

March 29

20___ ______________________________

____

____

____

20___ ______________________________

____

____

____

March 30

20___ ______________________________

____

____

____

20___ ______________________________

____

____

____

God, show me where You're working.

March 31

20___ ______________________________

____

____

____

20___ ______________________________

____

____

____

April 1

20___ ______________________________

____

____

____

20___ ______________________________

____

____

____

Help me to see You in everything, Lord.

April 2

20___ ______________________________

____

____

____

20___ ______________________________

____

____

____

April 3

20___ ______________________________

____

____

____

20___ ______________________________

____

____

____

God, show me where You're working.

April 4

20___ ______________________________

____

____

____

20___ ______________________________

____

____

____

April 5

20___ ______________________________

____

____

____

20___ ______________________________

____

____

____

Help me to see You in everything, Lord.

April 6

20___

20___

April 7

20___

20___

God, show me where You're working.

April 8

20___ ______________________________

____

____

____

20___ ______________________________

____

____

____

April 9

20___ ______________________________

____

____

____

20___ ______________________________

____

____

____

Help me to see You in everything, Lord.

April 10

20___ ___________________________________

____

____

____

20___ ___________________________________

____

____

____

April 11

20___ ___________________________________

____

____

____

20___ ___________________________________

____

____

____

God, show me where You're working.

April 12

20___ ________________________________

____

____

____

20___ ________________________________

____

____

____

April 13

20___ ________________________________

____

____

____

20___ ________________________________

____

____

____

Help me to see You in everything, Lord.

April 14

20___ ______________________________

____

____

____

20___ ______________________________

____

____

____

April 15

20___ ______________________________

____

____

____

20___ ______________________________

____

____

____

God, show me where You're working.

April 16

20___ ______________________________

____

____

____

20___ ______________________________

____

____

____

April 17

20___ ______________________________

____

____

____

20___ ______________________________

____

____

____

Help me to see You in everything, Lord.

April 18

20___ ____________________

20___ ____________________

April 19

20___ ____________________

20___ ____________________

God, show me where You're working.

April 20

20___ ______________________________

____

____

____

20___ ______________________________

____

____

____

April 21

20___ ______________________________

____

____

____

20___ ______________________________

____

____

____

Help me to see You in everything, Lord.

April 22

20___ ________________________________

____

____

____

20___ ________________________________

____

____

____

April 23

20___ ________________________________

____

____

____

20___ ________________________________

____

____

____

God, show me where You're working.

April 24

20___ ______________________________

____

____

____

20___ ______________________________

____

____

____

April 25

20___ ______________________________

____

____

____

20___ ______________________________

____

____

____

Help me to see You in everything, Lord.

April 26

20___ ___

___

___

___

20___ ___

___

___

___

April 27

20___ ___

___

___

___

20___ ___

___

___

___

God, show me where You're working.

April 28

20___ ______________________________

____

____

____

20___ ______________________________

____

____

____

April 29

20___ ______________________________

____

____

____

20___ ______________________________

____

____

____

Help me to see You in everything, Lord.

April 30

20___ ______________________________

____

____

____

20___ ______________________________

____

____

____

May 1

20___ ______________________________

____

____

____

20___ ______________________________

____

____

____

God, show me where You're working.

May 2

20___

20___

May 3

20___

20___

Help me to see You in everything, Lord.

May 4

20___ ______________________________

____

____

____

20___ ______________________________

____

____

____

May 5

20___ ______________________________

____

____

____

20___ ______________________________

____

____

____

God, show me where You're working.

May 6

20___ ______________________________

____

____

____

20___ ______________________________

____

____

____

May 7

20___ ______________________________

____

____

____

20___ ______________________________

____

____

____

Help me to see You in everything, Lord.

May 8

20___ ______________________________

____

____

____

20___ ______________________________

____

____

____

May 9

20___ ______________________________

____

____

____

20___ ______________________________

____

____

____

God, show me where You're working.

May 10

20___ ______________________________

____

____

____

20___ ______________________________

____

____

____

May 11

20___ ______________________________

____

____

____

20___ ______________________________

____

____

____

Help me to see You in everything, Lord.

May 12

20___

20___

May 13

20___

20___

God, show me where You're working.

May 14

20___ ______________________________

20___ ______________________________

May 15

20___ ______________________________

20___ ______________________________

Help me to see You in everything, Lord.

May 16

20___ ______________________________

____

____

____

20___ ______________________________

____

____

____

May 17

20___ ______________________________

____

____

____

20___ ______________________________

____

____

____

God, show me where You're working.

May 18

20___

20___

May 19

20___

20___

Help me to see You in everything, Lord.

May 20

20___ ______________________________

____

____

____

20___ ______________________________

____

____

____

May 21

20___ ______________________________

____

____

____

20___ ______________________________

____

____

____

God, show me where You're working.

May 22

20___

20___

May 23

20___

20___

Help me to see You in everything, Lord.

May 24

20___ ______________________________

20___ ______________________________

May 25

20___ ______________________________

20___ ______________________________

God, show me where You're working.

May 26

20___

20___

May 27

20___

20___

Help me to see You in everything, Lord.

May 28

20___

20___

May 29

20___

20___

God, show me where You're working.

May 30

20___ ______________________________

____

____

____

20___ ______________________________

____

____

____

May 31

20___ ______________________________

____

____

____

20___ ______________________________

____

____

____

Help me to see You in everything, Lord.

June 1

20___ ______________________________

____

____

____

20___ ______________________________

____

____

____

June 2

20___ ______________________________

____

____

____

20___ ______________________________

____

____

____

God, show me where You're working.

June 3

20___ ____________________

____

____

____

20___ ____________________

____

____

____

June 4

20___ ____________________

____

____

____

20___ ____________________

____

____

____

Help me to see You in everything, Lord.

June 5

20___

20___

June 6

20___

20___

God, show me where You're working.

June 7

20___ ____________________________

____

____

____

20___ ____________________________

____

____

____

June 8

20___ ____________________________

____

____

____

20___ ____________________________

____

____

____

Help me to see You in everything, Lord.

June 9

20___ ______________________________

____

____

____

20___ ______________________________

____

____

____

June 10

20___ ______________________________

____

____

____

20___ ______________________________

____

____

____

God, show me where You're working.

June 11

20___ ______________________________

____

____

____

20___ ______________________________

____

____

____

June 12

20___ ______________________________

____

____

____

20___ ______________________________

____

____

____

Help me to see You in everything, Lord.

June 13

20___ ______________________________

20___ ______________________________

June 14

20___ ______________________________

20___ ______________________________

God, show me where You're working.

June 15

20___ ______________________________

20___ ______________________________

June 16

20___ ______________________________

20___ ______________________________

Help me to see You in everything, Lord.

June 17

20___

20___

June 18

20___

20___

God, show me where You're working.

June 19

20___ ___________________________

____

____

____

20___ ___________________________

____

____

____

June 20

20___ ___________________________

____

____

____

20___ ___________________________

____

____

____

Help me to see You in everything, Lord.

June 21

20___ ______________________________

20___ ______________________________

June 22

20___ ______________________________

20___ ______________________________

God, show me where You're working.

June 23

20___

20___

June 24

20___

20___

Help me to see You in everything, Lord.

June 25

20___ ________________________________

____

____

____

20___ ________________________________

____

____

____

June 26

20___ ________________________________

____

____

____

20___ ________________________________

____

____

____

God, show me where You're working.

June 27

20___ ______________________________

____

____

____

20___ ______________________________

____

____

____

June 28

20___ ______________________________

____

____

____

20___ ______________________________

____

____

____

Help me to see You in everything, Lord.

I have hidden
your word
in my heart
that I might not
sin against
you.

Psalm 119:11

June 29

20___ ______________________________

____

____

____

20___ ______________________________

____

____

____

June 30

20___ ______________________________

____

____

____

20___ ______________________________

____

____

____

Help me to see You in everything, Lord.

July 1

20___

20___

July 2

20___

20___

God, show me where You're working.

July 3

20___

20___

July 4

20___

20___

Help me to see You in everything, Lord.

July 5

20___

20___

July 6

20___

20___

God, show me where You're working.

July 7

20___ ______________________________

____

____

____

20___ ______________________________

____

____

____

July 8

20___ ______________________________

____

____

____

20___ ______________________________

____

____

____

Help me to see You in everything, Lord.

July 9

20___ ____________________________________

____

____

____

20___ ____________________________________

____

____

____

July 10

20___ ____________________________________

____

____

____

20___ ____________________________________

____

____

____

God, show me where You're working.

July 11

20___ ______________________________

____

____

____

20___ ______________________________

____

____

____

July 12

20___ ______________________________

____

____

____

20___ ______________________________

____

____

____

Help me to see You in everything, Lord.

July 13

20___ ______________________________

20___ ______________________________

July 14

20___ ______________________________

20___ ______________________________

God, show me where You're working.

July 15

20___ ______________________________

____

____

____

20___ ______________________________

____

____

____

July 16

20___ ______________________________

____

____

____

20___ ______________________________

____

____

____

Help me to see You in everything, Lord.

July 17

20___ ______________________________

20___ ______________________________

July 18

20___ ______________________________

20___ ______________________________

God, show me where You're working.

July 19

20___ ______________________________

____

____

____

20___ ______________________________

____

____

____

July 20

20___ ______________________________

____

____

____

20___ ______________________________

____

____

____

Help me to see You in everything, Lord.

July 21

20___

20___

July 22

20___

20___

God, show me where You're working.

July 23

20___

20___

July 24

20___

20___

Help me to see You in everything, Lord.

July 25

20___ ______________________________

____

____

____

20___ ______________________________

____

____

____

July 26

20___ ______________________________

____

____

____

20___ ______________________________

____

____

____

God, show me where You're working.

July 27

20___ ______________________________

____

____

____

20___ ______________________________

____

____

____

July 28

20___ ______________________________

____

____

____

20___ ______________________________

____

____

____

Help me to see You in everything, Lord.

July 29

20___ ______________________________

20___ ______________________________

July 30

20___ ______________________________

20___ ______________________________

God, show me where You're working.

July 31

20___ ________________________________

____

____

____

20___ ________________________________

____

____

____

August 1

20___ ________________________________

____

____

____

20___ ________________________________

____

____

____

Help me to see You in everything, Lord.

August 2

20___ ___

20___ ___

August 3

20___ ___

20___ ___

God, show me where You're working.

August 4

20___ ______________________________

____

____

____

20___ ______________________________

____

____

____

August 5

20___ ______________________________

____

____

____

20___ ______________________________

____

____

____

Help me to see You in everything, Lord.

August 6

20___ ________________________________

____

____

____

20___ ________________________________

____

____

____

August 7

20___ ________________________________

____

____

____

20___ ________________________________

____

____

____

God, show me where You're working.

August 8

20___ ______________________________

____

____

____

20___ ______________________________

____

____

____

August 9

20___ ______________________________

____

____

____

20___ ______________________________

____

____

____

Help me to see You in everything, Lord.

August 10

20___ ___

20___ ___

August 11

20___ ___

20___ ___

God, show me where You're working.

For everything that
was written in the
past was written to
teach us, so that . . .
we might have hope.
Romans 15:4

August 12

20___

20___

August 13

20___

20___

God, show me where You're working.

August 14

20___

20___

August 15

20___

20___

Help me to see You in everything, Lord.

August 16

20___ ______________________________

20___ ______________________________

August 17

20___ ______________________________

20___ ______________________________

God, show me where You're working.

August 18

20___ ______________________________

____

____

____

20___ ______________________________

____

____

____

August 19

20___ ______________________________

____

____

____

20___ ______________________________

____

____

____

Help me to see You in everything, Lord.

August 20

20___ ______________________________

20___ ______________________________

August 21

20___ ______________________________

20___ ______________________________

God, show me where You're working.

August 22

20___

20___

August 23

20___

20___

Help me to see You in everything, Lord.

August 24

20___ ______________________________

____

____

____

20___ ______________________________

____

____

____

August 25

20___ ______________________________

____

____

____

20___ ______________________________

____

____

____

God, show me where You're working.

August 26

20___ ____________________

____

____

____

20___ ____________________

____

____

____

August 27

20___ ____________________

____

____

____

20___ ____________________

____

____

____

Help me to see You in everything, Lord.

August 28

20___ ______________________________

____

____

____

20___ ______________________________

____

____

____

August 29

20___ ______________________________

____

____

____

20___ ______________________________

____

____

____

God, show me where You're working.

August 30

20___ ______________________________

____

____

____

20___ ______________________________

____

____

____

August 31

20___ ______________________________

____

____

____

20___ ______________________________

____

____

____

Help me to see You in everything, Lord.

September 1

20___ ______________________________

____

____

____

20___ ______________________________

____

____

____

September 2

20___ ______________________________

____

____

____

20___ ______________________________

____

____

____

God, show me where You're working.

September 3

20___ ______________________________

____

____

____

20___ ______________________________

____

____

____

September 4

20___ ______________________________

____

____

____

20___ ______________________________

____

____

____

Help me to see You in everything, Lord.

September 5

20___ ______________________________

20___ ______________________________

September 6

20___ ______________________________

20___ ______________________________

God, show me where You're working.

September 7

20___ ________________________________

____

____

____

20___ ________________________________

____

____

____

September 8

20___ ________________________________

____

____

____

20___ ________________________________

____

____

____

Help me to see You in everything, Lord.

September 9

20___ ____________________

____

____

____

20___ ____________________

____

____

____

September 10

20___ ____________________

____

____

____

20___ ____________________

____

____

____

God, show me where You're working.

September 11

20___

20___

September 12

20___

20___

Help me to see You in everything, Lord.

September 13

20___ ________________________________

____

____

____

20___ ________________________________

____

____

____

September 14

20___ ________________________________

____

____

____

20___ ________________________________

____

____

____

God, show me where You're working.

September 15

20___ ______________________

____

____

____

20___ ______________________

____

____

____

September 16

20___ ______________________

____

____

____

20___ ______________________

____

____

____

Help me to see You in everything, Lord.

September 17

20___ ______________________________

____

____

____

20___ ______________________________

____

____

____

September 18

20___ ______________________________

____

____

____

20___ ______________________________

____

____

____

God, show me where You're working.

September 19

20___ ______________________________

____

____

____

20___ ______________________________

____

____

____

September 20

20___ ______________________________

____

____

____

20___ ______________________________

____

____

____

Help me to see You in everything, Lord.

September 21

20___

20___

September 22

20___

20___

God, show me where You're working.

September 23

20___ ______________________________

20___ ______________________________

September 24

20___ ______________________________

20___ ______________________________

Help me to see You in everything, Lord.

September 25

20___

20___

September 26

20___

20___

God, show me where You're working.

September 27

20___ ______________________________

____

____

____

20___ ______________________________

____

____

____

September 28

20___ ______________________________

____

____

____

20___ ______________________________

____

____

____

Help me to see You in everything, Lord.

Let the message
of Christ dwell
among you richly
as you teach and
admonish one
another with
all wisdom.

Colossians 3:16

September 29

20___ ____________________

____

____

____

20___ ____________________

____

____

____

September 30

20___ ____________________

____

____

____

20___ ____________________

____

____

____

Help me to see You in everything, Lord.

October 1

20___ ______________________________

____

____

____

20___ ______________________________

____

____

____

October 2

20___ ______________________________

____

____

____

20___ ______________________________

____

____

____

God, show me where You're working.

October 3

20___

20___

October 4

20___

20___

Help me to see You in everything, Lord.

October 5

20___ ______________________________

20___ ______________________________

October 6

20___ ______________________________

20___ ______________________________

God, show me where You're working.

October 7

20___ ______________________________

____

____

____

20___ ______________________________

____

____

____

October 8

20___ ______________________________

____

____

____

20___ ______________________________

____

____

____

Help me to see You in everything, Lord.

October 9

20___

20___

October 10

20___

20___

God, show me where You're working.

October 11

20___ ______________________________

____

____

____

20___ ______________________________

____

____

____

October 12

20___ ______________________________

____

____

____

20___ ______________________________

____

____

____

Help me to see You in everything, Lord.

October 13

20___ ______________________________

____

____

____

20___ ______________________________

____

____

____

October 14

20___ ______________________________

____

____

____

20___ ______________________________

____

____

____

God, show me where You're working.

October 15

20___ ______________________________

____

____

____

20___ ______________________________

____

____

____

October 16

20___ ______________________________

____

____

____

20___ ______________________________

____

____

____

Help me to see You in everything, Lord.

October 17

20___ ______________________________

20___ ______________________________

October 18

20___ ______________________________

20___ ______________________________

God, show me where You're working.

October 19

20___ ______________________________

____

____

____

20___ ______________________________

____

____

____

October 20

20___ ______________________________

____

____

____

20___ ______________________________

____

____

____

Help me to see You in everything, Lord.

October 21

20___ ______________________________

____

____

____

20___ ______________________________

____

____

____

October 22

20___ ______________________________

____

____

____

20___ ______________________________

____

____

____

God, show me where You're working.

October 23

20___ ______________________________

____

____

____

20___ ______________________________

____

____

____

October 24

20___ ______________________________

____

____

____

20___ ______________________________

____

____

____

Help me to see You in everything, Lord.

October 25

20___ ___

20___ ___

October 26

20___ ___

20___ ___

God, show me where You're working.

October 27

20___ ______________________________

____

____

____

20___ ______________________________

____

____

____

October 28

20___ ______________________________

____

____

____

20___ ______________________________

____

____

____

Help me to see You in everything, Lord.

October 29

20___ ___

20___ ___

October 30

20___ ___

20___ ___

God, show me where You're working.

October 31

20___ ______________________________

____

____

____

20___ ______________________________

____

____

____

November 1

20___ ______________________________

____

____

____

20___ ______________________________

____

____

____

Help me to see You in everything, Lord.

November 2

20___

20___

November 3

20___

20___

God, show me where You're working.

November 4

20___ ______________________________

____

____

____

20___ ______________________________

____

____

____

November 5

20___ ______________________________

____

____

____

20___ ______________________________

____

____

____

Help me to see You in everything, Lord.

November 6

20___ ______________________________

20___ ______________________________

November 7

20___ ______________________________

20___ ______________________________

God, show me where You're working.

November 8

20___

20___

November 9

20___

20___

Help me to see You in everything, Lord.

November 10

20___ ______________________________

____

____

____

20___ ______________________________

____

____

____

November 11

20___ ______________________________

____

____

____

20___ ______________________________

____

____

____

God, show me where You're working.

"For I know the plans I
have for you," declares the
Lord, "plans to prosper
you and not to harm
you, plans to give you
hope and a future."

Jeremiah 29:11

November 12

20___ ____________________________________

20___ ____________________________________

November 13

20___ ____________________________________

20___ ____________________________________

God, show me where You're working.

November 14

20___ ______________________________

____

____

____

20___ ______________________________

____

____

____

November 15

20___ ______________________________

____

____

____

20___ ______________________________

____

____

____

Help me to see You in everything, Lord.

November 16

20___ ______________________________

____

____

____

20___ ______________________________

____

____

____

November 17

20___ ______________________________

____

____

____

20___ ______________________________

____

____

____

God, show me where You're working.

November 18

20___

20___

November 19

20___

20___

Help me to see You in everything, Lord.

November 20

20___ ___________________________

____

____

____

20___ ___________________________

____

____

____

November 21

20___ ___________________________

____

____

____

20___ ___________________________

____

____

____

God, show me where You're working.

November 22

20___ ______________________________

____

____

____

20___ ______________________________

____

____

____

November 23

20___ ______________________________

____

____

____

20___ ______________________________

____

____

____

Help me to see You in everything, Lord.

November 24

20___ ______________________________

____

____

____

20___ ______________________________

____

____

____

November 25

20___ ______________________________

____

____

____

20___ ______________________________

____

____

____

God, show me where You're working.

November 26

20___ ____________________________

____

____

____

20___ ____________________________

____

____

____

November 27

20___ ____________________________

____

____

____

20___ ____________________________

____

____

____

Help me to see You in everything, Lord.

November 28

20___

20___

November 29

20___

20___

God, show me where You're working.

November 30

20___

20___

December 1

20___

20___

Help me to see You in everything, Lord.

December 2

20___ ______________________________

____

____

____

20___ ______________________________

____

____

____

December 3

20___ ______________________________

____

____

____

20___ ______________________________

____

____

____

God, show me where You're working.

December 4

20___ ___________________________

____

____

____

20___ ___________________________

____

____

____

December 5

20___ ___________________________

____

____

____

20___ ___________________________

____

____

____

Help me to see You in everything, Lord.

December 6

20___ ______________________________

____

____

____

20___ ______________________________

____

____

____

December 7

20___ ______________________________

____

____

____

20___ ______________________________

____

____

____

God, show me where You're working.

December 8

20___ ______________________________

____

____

____

20___ ______________________________

____

____

____

December 9

20___ ______________________________

____

____

____

20___ ______________________________

____

____

____

Help me to see You in everything, Lord.

Remember
the former things,
those of long ago;
I am God,
and there is
no other;
I am God,
and there is
none like me.

Isaiah 46:9

December 10

20___

20___

December 11

20___

20___

Help me to see You in everything, Lord.

December 12

20___ ______________________________

____

____

____

20___ ______________________________

____

____

____

December 13

20___ ______________________________

____

____

____

20___ ______________________________

____

____

____

God, show me where You're working.

December 14

20___ ______________________________

____

____

____

20___ ______________________________

____

____

____

December 15

20___ ______________________________

____

____

____

20___ ______________________________

____

____

____

Help me to see You in everything, Lord.

December 16

20___ ______________________________

____

____

____

20___ ______________________________

____

____

____

December 17

20___ ______________________________

____

____

____

20___ ______________________________

____

____

____

God, show me where You're working.

December 18

20___ ______________________________

____

____

____

20___ ______________________________

____

____

____

December 19

20___ ______________________________

____

____

____

20___ ______________________________

____

____

____

Help me to see You in everything, Lord.

December 20

20___ ______________________________

____

____

____

20___ ______________________________

____

____

____

December 21

20___ ______________________________

____

____

____

20___ ______________________________

____

____

____

God, show me where You're working.

December 22

20___ ________________________________

____

____

____

20___ ________________________________

____

____

____

December 23

20___ ________________________________

____

____

____

20___ ________________________________

____

____

____

Help me to see You in everything, Lord.

December 24

20___

20___

December 25

20___

20___

God, show me where You're working.

December 26

20___ ______________________________

____

____

____

20___ ______________________________

____

____

____

December 27

20___ ______________________________

____

____

____

20___ ______________________________

____

____

____

Help me to see You in everything, Lord.

December 28

20___ ______________________________

____

____

____

20___ ______________________________

____

____

____

December 29

20___ ______________________________

____

____

____

20___ ______________________________

____

____

____

God, show me where You're working.

December 30

20___ ______________________________

____

____

____

20___ ______________________________

____

____

____

December 31

20___ ______________________________

____

____

____

20___ ______________________________

____

____

____

Help me to see You in everything, Lord.

Jesus did many other
things as well. If every one
of them were written down,
I suppose that even the
whole world would not
have room for the books
that would be written.

John 21:25

Special Dates

Date: ______________________________

What Made It Special: ______________________________

____

Date: ______________________________

What Made It Special: ______________________________

____

Date: ______________________________

What Made It Special: ______________________________

____

Date: ______________________________

What Made It Special: ______________________________

____

Date: ______________________________

What Made It Special: ______________________________

____

Special Dates

Date: ____________________________

What Made It Special: ______________________

____

Date: ____________________________

What Made It Special: ______________________

____

Date: ____________________________

What Made It Special: ______________________

____

Date: ____________________________

What Made It Special: ______________________

____

Date: ____________________________

What Made It Special: ______________________

____